SOUL BROTHERS

SOUL BROTHERS

Men in the Bible
Speak to Men Today

RICHARD ROHR

Art by
LOUIS GLANZMAN

ORBIS BOOKS

Maryknoll, New York 10545

Second Printing, October 2004

Founded in 1970, Orbis Books endeavors to publish works that enlighten the mind, nourish the spirit, and challenge the conscience. The publishing arm of the Maryknoll Fathers and Brothers, Orbis seeks to explore the global dimensions of the Christian faith and mission, to invite dialogue with diverse cultures and religious traditions, and to serve the cause of reconciliation and peace. The books published reflect the views of their authors and do not represent the official position of the Maryknoll Society. To learn more about Maryknoll and Orbis Books, please visit our website at www.maryknoll.org.

Library of Congress Cataloging-in-Publication Data

Rohr, Richard.
    Soul brothers : men in the Bible speak to men today / Richard Rohr ;
art by Louis Glanzman.
       p. cm.
    ISBN 1-57075-534-5 (pbk.)
    1. Men in the Bible—Meditations. 2. Christian men—Prayer-books and
devotions—English. I. Title.
BS574.5 .R64 2004
220.9'2'081—dc22
                                            2003019855

Contents

Preface · vii

Abraham · 1
The Father of All Faithfulness

Moses · 13
The Man Who Argues with God and Wins

David · 23
From Forgotten Son to Remembered King

Isaiah · 33
Teaching by Creating the Tension

John the Baptist · 43
The First Necessary Freedom

Peter · 53
He Came to God by Doing It Wrong

Paul · 63
A Man of Contradictions

Timothy · 75
A Beginner's Mind

Contents

John the Evangelist · 85
The Pain and Poverty of Chosenness

Elijah · 95
Just Enough to Get Your Attention

Joseph · 105
Man of Dreams

Jesus · 115
The Human One

Preface

When I first looked at Louis Glanzman's paintings of biblical women in the book *Soul Sisters*, I saw beauty, strength, wisdom, and courage; and Edwina Gateley's poetic text was deeply moving to me. I didn't think much more about it until publisher Mike Leach called to tell me that the artist had finished twelve portraits of biblical men. Would I like to see them?

Since I had been working with men and studying male spirituality for twenty years, I was eager to see the portraits. When I did, I again perceived beauty, strength, wisdom, and courage, and no small measure of gratitude and love. Louis Glanzman's art is to reveal the very soul of an individual. When Mike asked me to write the text to accompany this artwork in a new book, I felt challenged and apprehensive but said I would give it a try.

It was an amazing experience. The words flowed non-stop, quickly, joyously, and without effort. It was for me the exciting difference between *doing* something and *being used* to do something. I wrote the text during a Lenten hermitage in Arizona in 2003 where I used the portraits for meditation. They inspired me to put on paper some of the most courageous scriptural work I have ever done.

I hope the Spirit will use my words to inspire the same courage and confidence in others. I am sure the paintings will.

This book is not just for men and not just for Christians. I hope it will be helpful to anyone involved in the human struggle. I do hope that men, in particular, will find their spirituality enriched through these men in the Bible with whom we have all grown up but whom we perhaps have seldom taken to heart as imitable or even believable models. This book is an invitation to let their souls touch our own.

I am grateful to Louis Glanzman, Orbis Books, my Scripture teachers, these wonderful/terrible twelve men, and especially that "ultimate flow" called the Holy Spirit.

RICHARD ROHR
ALBUQUERQUE, NEW MEXICO

SOUL BROTHERS

Abraham

The Father of All Faithfulness

It happened some time later that the word of Yahweh was spoken to Abram in a vision, "Have no fear, Abram, for I am your shield. Your reward will be very great."

"My Lord, Yahweh," Abram replied, "what do you intend to give me? I am childless."

Then taking him outside, Yahweh said, "Look up to the heavens and count the stars if you can. Such will be your descendants. . . ."

And as the sun was setting Abram fell into a deep sleep, and terror seized him . . . and when the sun set and darkness had fallen, there appeared a smoking furnace and a firebrand that moved between the halved animals [of sacrifice]. That day Yahweh made a covenant with Abram.

Genesis 15:1-2, 5, 12, 17

A primeval story. A primal man. So much so, that it becomes a founding myth for all three monotheistic religions —but really quite amazing, since it has nothing to do with a hero in any classical sense. There is no great adventure here, no conquering of lands, monsters, or villains. Abraham does nothing special at all. To the typical male it is a quick read, and maybe more than a bit disappointing. Abraham's glory is not in his giving or conquering or achieving, but totally in his receiving and nonachieving. He might be called a patriarch, but this story is rather unpatriarchal. In fact, this patriarch is even willing to kill the centerpiece of all patriarchy— the son who would inherit it all. What is going on here? Why would this anti-story so capture the religious imagination of Jews, Christians, and Muslims together?

While we consider some elements of the several accounts about Abraham in Genesis, let us keep an eye on our portrait: a man facing left or backward rather than the typical manly pose facing right and forward. Note also the little ram caught in the thicket.

I am told that the history of religion has run parallel to the history of violence. We always needed some guise to take away our guilt about killing, and God turned out to be the best cover possible. Just kill for God, and it is all right. Then you can remain hateful and self-centered, but actually think of yourself as saved and superior. Historians of religion say that there is evidence of human sacrifice on every continent if you go back far enough. Virgin daughters were thrown into Mayan wells, and eldest sons in the Bible were sacrificed to rally the fighting spirit of the hometown team (see 2 Kings 3:26-27 for a perfect example of the power of sacrificial killing). The sacrificial or heroic instinct lies very deep in the human psyche. For some reason, we believe that God can be persuaded or bought off by various forms of gratuitous killing. It makes one wonder what we think of God? The only reason the story of Abraham and Isaac can be told at all is that fathers did kill sons to placate an angry, distant, and scary god. Except in the view of the mystics of every age, God has not been a very likable person in most of history.

The violence moved from human sacrifice to animal sacrifice ("rams caught in thickets"), which is where we are at the time of the Bible. Cultural anthropologists estimate that as much as 90 percent of the economy of the city of Jerusalem at the time of Jesus had to do with the buying, penning, feeding, herding, and butchering of sacrificial animals and with hauling their dead carcasses out of the temple. Humans believed they were paying off some kind of huge debt to a god who kept them perpetually in debtors' prison. Sacrifices satisfied that tit-for-tat need, that mercantile instinct, which is how the dualistic mind operates until its logic is broken down by unearned gratuity. No wonder Jesus said so strongly, "Go learn the meaning of the words, what I want is mercy and not sacrifices" (Matthew 9:13). And the centuries seem to have shouted back to him, "But what we want is sacrifices and not mercy!"

I guess you could consider it to be some level of human development, but later centuries largely transferred the notion of sacrifice to ideas of a heroic self. If we were ascetic, abstemious, mortified, and anal retentive, this was supposed to win God's favor, for some reason. It took the form of Stoicism, Manichaeism, Jansenism, Puritanism, Victorian duty, and black-and-white moralisms of every stripe. Anything rather than receive God's obvious love as a free gift. Anything rather than the erotic language of the bride and bridegroom, the wedding banquet of rich wine, the intimate encounters of the mystics, a religion based on communion instead of fear. "The Son of Man comes eating and drinking, and you say, 'Look, a glutton and a drunkard, a friend of tax collectors and sinners,'" says Jesus (Matthew 11:19). How did Christianity end up so utterly different from Jesus? becomes the disturbing question after a few years of studying the New Testament.

Well, one answer might be that we forgot about Abraham, whose "faith is the father of us all" (Romans 4:1, 16). As Paul goes on at great length to teach (the rest of Romans 4), Abraham's faith was the exact opposite of any kind of performance principle. Or, as Hebrews puts it, "Abraham obeyed the call to set out for a country that was merely promised to him as an inheritance, and he set out without knowing where he was going. . . . They lived there in tents, while he looked forward to a city founded, designed, and built by God" (11:8, 10). Now this is a genuinely new notion of religion! No ego payoffs. This religion meant living in the "in-betweens" of life, energized by the experience of one God, waiting in confidence and hope for a God who seems distant and demanding. This is considerably different from the prosperity gospel and "prayer-of-Jabez" (1 Chronicles 4:10) kind of religion that we tout today. Strangely, we end up with no sacrifices demanded of anybody—except perhaps for the underdeveloped countries who have to subsidize our Cadillac faith, our oil wars, and our pretentiousness.

History ping-pongs from one extreme to the other, either moral asceticism or religious imperialism, but both are a refusal to trust in the goodness and faithfulness of God; we try instead to trust in our own. Both extremes avoid and fear the transformative "terror," "darkness," and "setting sun" that are referred to deliberately in Genesis. We see it in Abraham's half-closed eyes and graying beard in our Glanzman portrait. Abraham is not a man who is afraid of hell, like so many modern Christians—what we see is a man who has been through hell. Those hellish journeys allowed him to receive the gifts and promises of God in freedom and desire.

Until we are led to the limits of our own resources, we do not know what our Real Resource is. Yahweh does not tell Abraham that he will not be tried or tested; Yahweh simply says to Abraham: "Do not be afraid. I will be your shield" (Genesis 15:1). That is a very different message from such statements of "ascent" as "I will do it by will power, effort, and good works" or "I will use my religion to hold sway over others." Abraham's religion is all surrender, trust, and letting go—a path of descent not ascent, subtraction not addition.

According to Ken Wilber (*One Taste* [Boston: Shambala, 2000], journal entry of February 11), religion has always performed two very important but very different functions, but most people stop after the first and never go on to the second. The first function of religion is that it gives meaning, boundaries, and identity to the private self. This is good and necessary to get one started on the religious journey. We see the same approach to religion in much of Leviticus, Numbers, and Deuteronomy. It is the important first stage of knowing that you are chosen, special, and even set apart. Psychologically, you have to have an ego before you can let go of your ego. Yahweh satisfies that human need for a "narcissistic fix" by telling Abraham that his descendants will be as many as the stars of the heavens and the sands of the seashore. "I will bless you and make your name so famous that it will be used as a blessing" (Genesis 12:2). First God inflates you, so that you can handle the later and necessary deflation. God lets you know that you are a beloved son or daughter, and then God gives you the freedom to choose it and believe it consciously, which is always through some form of terror, darkness, or setting sun.

But the second function of religion, according to Wilber, is the real goal, the second half of life's clear task. It is usually lived by a small minority of every religion or denomination, he says. It is Jesus' "narrow path that few walk upon," his way of descent, the picking up of our cross and entering into solidarity with him and humanity. Here the task is not affirmation of the ego but surrender of the ego, not self-control but giving up control, not flattering exclusivity but humiliating inclusivity. It is not about winning but about losing, not "I am good" but "God is good"—not sacrifices but mercy. This is the full and complete Abrahamic journey, and it will always be a minority position, not a state religion. The monotheistic religions were correct in their intuition about the archetypal nature of Abraham. But when they tried to mass-produce it, membership in a group became more important than participation in a real journey of transformation.

We see Abraham's transformed self most beautifully represented in the final stages of his saga, when he and Sarah are "well on in years." First we see that he has become the essence of hospitality; he "hastens," "bows," and "runs" to serve the three strangers in the heat of the day at Mamre (Genesis 18)—more feminine than patriarchal, it seems. He then guides and accompanies them like a humble servant on their mission to Sodom, and only then does he discover that two of them are angels and one is actually Yahweh in disguise! This becomes the key text for that ever-surprising discovery of "entertaining angels unaware," which is actually the story of our whole life.

Finally, we have the almost shocking story of Abraham haggling and bargaining to keep Yahweh from destroying Sodom. It risks making Abraham look more loving and merciful than God! And what is more, Yahweh relents to Abraham's final offer, "I will not destroy the city for the sake of even ten just men" (Genesis 18:32), God says. It is the beginning of the unfolding and surprising theme of the remnant, the minyan, the salt of the earth, and the yeast hidden inside the dough. It seems that God just needs a few willing partners to assist in the redemption of the world. The Great Lover needs only a few conscious lovers to join in a giant yes to life. It is these ecstatic ones, these few who bother to answer the invitation, who seem to be enough to turn the world from its path toward mutual and self-destruction. These are the sons and daughters of Abraham "raised up from the very stones" of creation instead of any religious lineage or group (Matthew 3:9). All God needs, it seems, is a critical mass or, as Jesus puts it, "two or three gathered in my name" (Matthew 18:20).

Abraham did not finally argue with God because he imagined that he himself was good and merciful. He argued with God because he had learned that God was good and merciful. Such full-circle faith will always save us from the need to create sacrifices and scapegoats. Abraham does not even need that poor ram caught in the thicket. He looks straight ahead to life, sandy seashores, and stars uncountable.

*M*oses

The Man Who Argues with God and Wins

Yahweh said, "Go on to the land where milk and honey flow. But I shall not go with you myself—you are a head-strong people—and I might exterminate you on the way." On hearing these stern words, the people went into mourning. . . .

But Yahweh would speak with Moses face to face, as a man speaks with his friend. . . .

And Moses said to Yahweh, "See, you yourself say to me, 'Make the people go on,' but you never let me know who it is you will send with me. . . . If indeed you know me well and you are pleased with me, then let me know of what nature you are, so that I can understand you and please you. Remember, also, that this nation is your own people."

And Yahweh replied, "I myself will go with you, and I

will give you security. . . . I will do what you have asked,
because I am pleased with you and I know you face to
face."

Exodus 33:3, 11-13, 17

You could not look directly into Moses' eyes; they were shadowed by his veil. One cannot look directly into the eyes that have seen God and live in the normal world ever again. For the rest of Moses' life, "the skin on his face was radiant after speaking with Yahweh" (34:29); and so he put a veil over his face, only removing it when he returned to speak with God. Most of his headstrong people were not ready for Moses' inner experience, and they fought him nonstop every step of the journey (see Exodus 14:11-12). Yet he never stopped leading them. That is the tension and the dynamic of Moses' entire life. He was a pastor, a prophet, and a true priest all at once, which is most rare. Not only did he hold the people together in life as a pastor does, but he led them beyond their easy comfort zones as a prophet does, and as a priest he made the inner connections and transformations of soul that kept them face to face with God.

Eyes really are, as Jesus says, "the lamp of the body" (Matthew 6:22). How you see is what you see. "If your eye is sound, your whole body will be filled with light. But if your eye is diseased, your whole body will be darkness." I think we could follow Moses' entire development in terms of his learning how to see. This learning began with seeing God's true nature (Exodus 33:13) and daring to look at God "face to face." It had the effect of making others unable to look at Moses, because, as Paul says, "we reflect like mirrors the brightness of the Lord, all growing brighter and brighter as we are turned into the image that we reflect; this is the work of the Lord who is Spirit" (2 Corinthians 3:18). Both Moses and Paul became the one they loved, which is, of course, true for all of us.

Humans grow in the presence of those who respect them. They even grow *for* those who respect them. In fact, the English word "respect" means to "look again." It is very hard to look into someone else's eyes directly or for very long, and it is almost impossible to look into the eyes of someone with whom you are angry or someone from whom you are alienated. But when we can dare to look again, and again, when we can risk being looked *at* again, and again, the lamp of the body does its work and our whole body is filled with light.

No wonder the people thought Moses had "horns" proceeding from his face. Contemporary studies and heat-sensitive photography of the heart–brain connection prove that there is indeed an aura or halo that proceeds from truly loving and godly people. Religion's intuitions are invariably correct.

That same photography can show that hateful and negative people not only have no aura around them, but they actually draw energy out of others. That is what the people of Israel must have done to Moses and Jesus too, and why they are always retreating to be with the pure Source of Light. "Show me your effulgence, I beg you," says Moses, as he stands in the cleft of the rock asking for God to pass by (Exodus 33:18-23). Here he still cannot see the face of God, but in a most daring passage, even "the back" of God is enough to en-lighten him and is itself too much for him.

I think that Moses and God "respected" each other. They looked back and forth many times and never avoided the gaze for long—which is when the alienation and mistrust always set in. But, as always, God has taken the initiative in this respectful relationship with Moses. He invited this fleeing murderer (Exodus 2:12-15) into an amazing solitary intimacy. It is an experience that Moses describes as "a blazing bush that does not burn up." He is caught between running forward into it and coming no nearer and taking off his shoes (Exodus 3:2)—the classic *mysterium tremendum*. It is common for mystics, from Moses to Bonaventure, Philip Neri, and Pascal, to describe the experience of God as fire or a furnace or pure light. But at this early experience "Moses covered his face, afraid to look back at God" (Exodus 3:6). He had to be slowly taught how to look back. For now, he still lived like all of us, in his shame.

God slowly has to convince Moses of his respect, which Moses calls "favor," but not without some serious objections from Moses' side. It is a long fight, but, as we know, God always wins in fights with humans. Almost immediately after the experience of the blazing bush comes the political commission to confront the pharaoh of Egypt and tell him to stop oppressing the enslaved Hebrews. This is the foundational text for teaching the essential linkage between spirituality and social engagement, prayer and politics, contemplation and action. It stands at the exact beginning of the Judeo-Christian tradition; but the connection is constantly forgotten or denied, and it is the job of the prophets and Jesus to remake the essential connection. Moses takes spirituality and social engagement together from the very beginning.

In response to Yahweh, Moses quickly comes up with five objections: (1) "Who am I?" (2) "Who are you?" (3) "What if they do not believe me?" (4) "I stutter." And (5) "Why not send someone else?" If it were not the classic biblical text that it is, I would think it to be a cartoon in the *New Yorker!* In each case, God stays in the dialogue, answering Moses respectfully and even intimately, only offering a promise of personal Presence, and an ever-sustaining glimpse into who God is—Being Itself, Existence Itself, a nameless God beyond all names, a formless God previous to all forms, a liberator God who is utterly liberated. God asserts God's ultimate freedom from human attempts to capture God in concepts and words by saying, "I am who I am" (Exodus 3:14). What we will see is that Moses slowly absorbs this same daring freedom.

But to learn it, Yahweh has to assign Moses a specific task: to create freedom *for* people who don't want it very badly, and freedom *from* an oppressor who thinks he is totally in control. It is in working for outer freedom, peace, and justice in the world that we have to discover an even deeper inner freedom to survive in the presence of so much death. Most people become cynical and angry and retreat into various ideological theories over time. Or they just walk away and return to an indulgent liberal worldview—this happened to much of my own generation of the 1960s. Again, we see the inherent connection between action and contemplation, the dialogue between the outer journey and the inner journey. Moses is almost a perfect paradigm of the same.

Moses stayed with the headstrong Hebrews until some of them finally crossed the Jordan. When Moses died and was buried on the east side of the river, "his eyes were undimmed and his vigor unimpaired" (Deuteronomy 34:7). It is, of course, totally unnecessary for Moses to cross over or to "descend into reality" any further (Jordan means "descent"). The Promised Land is not a piece of real estate but an inner dwelling place that creates our outer worlds. Yahweh's final words to Moses were, "Die on the mountain you have climbed" (Deuteronomy 32:50). We all do anyway, in one sense or another.

Henceforth, the preferred metaphors of the Jewish prophets for the spiritual journey are not those of the legal system but instead those of the marriage relationship: bride and bridegroom, faithfulness, and espousal. Sin is also described in personal terms as prostitution and adultery. Only sexual imagery is strong enough to communicate the mutual desire and the reciprocal gaze back and forth. In the lovely Song of Moses toward the end of Deuteronomy, Moses presents Yahweh as a truly "jealous" lover (32:16, 21) and he himself as one who has been penetrated by God's passion, "Is he not something precious to me, sealed inside my treasury?" (32:34). The two faces have become one love, which is what happens at the end of all true love affairs. The mutual "respect" of the lovers is sealed in what soon becomes the precious language of covenant.

And "since then, never has there been such a prophet in Israel as Moses, the man who knew Yahweh face to face" (Deuteronomy 33:10).

avid

*From Forgotten Son
to Remembered King*

*The prophet Samuel said to Jesse, "Are these all the sons
that you have?"*

*Jesse answered, "Oh, there is still one left. He is the
youngest. He is out watching the sheep."*

*And Samuel said, "Send for him. We will not eat until
he comes."*

*And a boy of fresh complexion, with fine eyes, and
pleasant bearing came in from the fields.*

And Yahweh said, "Come, anoint him. He is the one!"

1 Samuel 16:11-12

Well, there it all is! The entire biblical tradition of free election, the choice of the "least," charism over office, no

requirements for worthiness, no theophany or church service, all the training coming apparently after the fact—and we are supposed to take such a God seriously! And take this young recruit seriously too, which we only gradually do. We watch him grow into a man and a king in front of our eyes.

Good old Jesse of Bethlehem has just trotted out all of his seven sons in front of the prophet Samuel, sort of like Cinderella's sisters trying on the glass slipper. In fact, a story like *Cinderella* may have originated in a culture that was formed on images like these. But in this primitive story, David is "Cinderfellow" and gets to go to the ball. Thus the saga begins and produces the ultimate Jewish whole man, David. So much so, that even Jesus, the Christian whole man, is first described as coming from "the house of David" (Luke 2:27, 32). David, like the ultimate American ideal, started at the bottom and made it to the top.

I like this portrait of David because it shows him in these honest and humble beginnings. Not an idealized version by Michelangelo, not with his foot tromping Goliath, but a mere shepherd boy, just old enough to sport a beard and mustache, and tender enough to care for a small lamb. Not a man who is born to be king, but a man who is slowly initiated into kingship. In the short space that this meditation allows, let's try to trace his male and royal initiation step by step.

I would like to draw on the scholarship of Robert Moore and Douglas Gillette here (*King, Warrior, Magician, Lover: Rediscovering the Archetypes of the Mature Masculine* [San Francisco: HarperSanFrancisco, 1991]). I believe they have done both mythology and Sacred Scripture a great favor in pointing out these four roles, which recur in almost all male stories and legends. They are never more obvious than in the biblical presentation of the character of David.

David is providentially drawn into the royal court when poor King Saul has an evil spirit and is looking for someone who can play healing music for him (1 Samuel 16:17). Saul sounds like Amfortas, the Fisher King, presiding over the wasteland. A soldier describes to Saul a shepherd boy from Bethlehem (note how all four parts of a man's soul are already apparent in this one-verse description of David): "He is a skilled player [lover], a brave man and a fighter [warrior]; he is prudent in speech and a man of presence [wise man or magus], and Yahweh is with him [sacred king]" (1 Samuel

16:18). This sounds like a winning résumé for *The Dating Game*. Much of the rest of the saga of David concerns his struggle with the shadow side of each aspect of his personality, which is precisely the journey to wholeness and holiness. David is a textbook *Mensch,* a boy destined to be king (which is all of us, by the way).

We all know the "Lover Archetype" in David, since that is the juicy part that makes for good film and memorable reading. Apparently he plays the harp well; he was credited with writing as many as 82 of the 150 Psalms; he dances obscenely and ecstatically before the Ark of the Covenant and either shocks or delights the maidens (2 Samuel 6:14-23); he "sings to the accompaniment of lyres, harps, tambourines, castanets, and cymbals" (2 Samuel 6:5); he composes a moving elegy and lament over both Saul and Jonathan, one whom he had every reason to hate, and the other whom he seemed to love in an almost homoerotic way (2 Samuel 1:17-27); he weeps profusely at the death of his son Absalom and also at the death of Bathsheba's child (2 Samuel 19:1-4; 12:16-23); he has intense compassion for

Meribbaal, the crippled son of Jonathan, and lets him eat at his table forever (2 Samuel 9:1-13); and we all know about his passionate encounter with Bathsheba, which is almost his undoing—not because of the adultery but because of his evil attempt to cover it up by having her husband, Uriah, killed (2 Samuel 11–12). David has many wives and lots of children.

Each of these stories is so compelling and alive even today, that I would say that David's primary archetype is clearly lover. He wants to "taste everything" fully. He lives his life 120 percent, which is both his gift and almost his undoing. It is his struggle with his pan-eroticism that undoubtedly brings him to final consciousness, humility, and surrender. As always, his gift is also his sin and his sin becomes his gift.

David is also clearly the "Warrior Archetype." He starts by being Saul's armor bearer, but soon surpasses him in battle, so that the women sing: "Saul has killed his thousands, but David his tens of thousands" (1 Samuel 18:7). David is able to evade Saul's numerous attempts to kill him, and he reverses Saul's failed attempt to spear him (1 Samuel 18:10-11) by taking Saul's own spear from his side while he sleeps—but he refuses to kill "God's anointed" because of respect for his role (1 Samuel 26). The story of David's heroic killing of Goliath the Philistine with a slingshot (1 Samuel 17) is the stuff of every boy's dreams, but it also shows the Jewish admiration for the "little guy" who wins. In general, David's fastings, his rigorous campaigns in wilderness settings, his self-discipline, his ability to defer to the king and admit when he is wrong all show the virtues of the warrior. He knows boundaries, but he defends boundaries, even at great cost to himself. He is really a classic warrior, with even the first hints of nonviolence, when he could use power but chooses not to. The beginnings of the good warrior are in David.

This David is finally a king for forty years. Robert Moore says that one cannot really access the King Archetype much before the age of fifty, and maybe that explains David's earlier mistakes and why it took him a while to put all of the parts together. (This is honest hagiography, as opposed to the sanitized lives of saints that Catholics are usually subjected to.) The "king" in you honors, holds together, and regulates every other part to create a balanced wholeness: lover, warrior, and magician move together as one, which is why it takes so long to become a good king and a "grand"-father. You have to have loved, failed, sinned, and been forgiven a number of times to understand the mystery of life. You have to understand power in very refined ways and the different forms that it takes in each part of your soul. "Power is not bad," says the king. It just needs to be tamed and integrated for the common good. If anything, we need more of such power.

Psychologically and spiritually David became the king of Israel when he both honored and protected the kingship of Saul, even though Saul was trying to kill him. The king is that part of you that holds its power so securely that it does not even have to use it. It can love and forgive its enemies, as we see in Jesus, the "King of kings." David's unquestioned relationship with God makes him also a "sacred king," who holds together heaven and earth. 2 Samuel 8:15 sums it up: "David ruled over all Israel, administering law and justice to all his people." The king holds all realms together in one pleasing Camelot because he has first of all held it together inside of himself. When the head is healthy, the whole kingdom flourishes. And when the fish rots, it starts with the head.

$$\sim\hspace{-0.5em}\sim$$

But you say, Where is the magus or wise man? To be honest, he is less visible than the other three archetypes in David. There is always one that we resist and do not fully appreciate or access. If and when we can, we are whole and hold the generative energy of a king-grandfather. As I see it, the prophets Samuel and Nathan symbolize the missing part of David. When he accepts their word, their anointings, their warnings, and their punishments, he accesses the whole "realm" of his soul. He is *real*, which not coincidentally, at least in Spanish, means royal. There is one lesser-known passage that says David went to live "in the huts of Ramah" with Samuel. The atmosphere sounds almost shamanic and ecstatic in what was a "school for prophets" (1 Samuel 19:18-24). The giveaway is that when he leaves, he runs straight to his best friend, Jonathan, with new words of awareness: "What have I done, what is my guilt, and what is my sin?" The precise role of the magician is always to get you to confront your grandiosity and your dark side. When the wise man or the prophet is missing from the story, the shadow side of things is always out of control, as in much of America today, where we do not honor true wisdom or truth. It is probably safe to say that the wise man is also "the missing quadrant" in the American psyche today (which means the king is also absent).

Through two prophets the summary message is given at the beginning and toward the end of David's life: Yahweh says through Samuel, "This is the one!" (1 Samuel 16:12), and through Nathan, "You are the man!" (2 Samuel 12:7). They are both right. He is.

Isaiah

Teaching by Creating the Tension

"Go, and say to this people, 'Hear and hear again, but do not understand; see and see again, but do not perceive.' Make the heart of this people gross, its ears dull. Shut its eyes so that it will not see with its eyes, hear with its ears, understand with its heart, and be converted and healed."

I answered, "But, until when, Lord?"

He answered: "Until towns have been laid waste and deserted, houses left untenanted, countryside made desolate, and Yahweh drives the people out. There must be a great emptiness in the country. With only a tenth of the people remaining, it will be stripped like a terebinth tree, so that only the stock remains. And this stock will be a holy seed."

Isaiah 6:9-13

Most scholars agree that at least three individual writers from three distinct historical periods composed the work we know as the Book of Isaiah. We are going to rely on the eighth-century Jerusalem prophet who first gave the name Isaiah its glory. Later prophets put his name to their works to assure that they would be taken seriously. We are going to take "First" Isaiah seriously for his own sake. He was not just the quintessential Jewish prophet; he was both a social and a religious critic, a man of his times, an eloquent writer and poet, a teacher of what we would now call "nonviolent resistance," and a man whose faithfulness earned him the right to call others to the same. He is sometimes simply called the Prophet of Faith, and his work almost defines the very term.

Like all great religious figures, Isaiah is best understood in light of the nature of his initial religious encounter. How we first break through, or how God breaks through to us, seems not just to mark a person indelibly; it determines how and what one sees as important for the rest of one's life. Isaiah's original "theophany" becomes the imprinting that never leaves his eyes: God is transcendent beauty and we are "as dust on the scales." That absolute center allows him to call all passing things into question: liturgy, priestcraft, kings of his own nation and other nations, political alliances, national security, the rich and powerful, and social injustice in general. The "smoke-filled" temple surrounding the vision (Isaiah 6:1-13) becomes his own "cloud of unknowing," which leads him into a holy skepticism about all things except the "Holy One of Israel."

If God alone is holy, then we are not. If God alone is worthy, then why do we keep trying to prove our own value by debt codes (temple requirements to achieve ritual purity) and purity codes? "I am a man of unclean lips, and I live among a people of unclean lips," Isaiah says (6:5). Yet he can risk saying, "Here I am, send me!" (6:9). Holiness, for Isaiah, is not a moral concept or a ritual purity. It is something that he knows only in comparison and contrast to the wholeness of God. If you don't know God, you don't know what sin is. Whatever God is, is what holiness is. It includes justice, honesty, compassion, and mercy, but is far greater than the sum of all these parts. Perhaps one reason religion becomes so brittle and legalistic is that it normally tries to define sin as an abstract concept apart from the authentic experience of God. Isaiah never does.

———

But then his first instructions, which we read above, seem downright disturbing. Yahweh appears to be saying that his job is to "create the problem" or even close people down. Isaiah himself is confused and says, "How long will it be like this, Lord?" (6:9-11). But the answer is even more enigmatic and demanding. Yahweh says that until this people is whittled down like a stripped terebinth tree, which must be "felled" with only the stump remaining, there will not be a "holy seed" from which to grow anew (6:12-13). This becomes the enduring theme of the purified remnant, the small refined group that God needs to save history. It is very different from our individualistic notion of personal salvation. It remains a central theme of Isaiah and of almost every prophet following him; it is seen in Jesus' choice of the seventy-two, the twelve, and then the three, and it continues in Paul. The prophet's task is very modest and almost disappointing—not the creating of religious empire or "Christendom" but the creating of a *usable quorum* for God.

This same instruction is quoted by Jesus to illustrate why he teaches in parables (Matthew 13:14-15). It is because parables are a brilliant form of soft "deconstruction" of one's comfortable biases, worldviews, and self-importance. They are one of Jesus' ways of being prophetic. Isaiah seems to prefer a more straightforward and "hard" deconstruction of both temple and society. But listen closely—I don't think he ever expected the kings of Judah to agree with him when he told them not to form alliances with Assyria or Egypt but to trust in God, but he *had* to say it! Isaiah saw world events as a staging area through which enduring truth could be captured, an arena for human transformation and for God's "glory to fill the whole earth" (6:3).

Prophets are totally on God's side when they talk to the people, and totally on the people's side when they talk to God. They are the ultimate go-betweens, and they seem to see themselves as standing in the gap. Prophets teach the Jewish version of the Buddhist "first principle of impermanence." The Dalai Lama, for example, accepts that his beloved Tibet, like everything else, must rise and then vanish, which is a great disappointment to those shouting "Free Tibet!" Yet the Dalai Lama would still agree that someone must also work to "Free Tibet"; his job is to say "It is still all right." That is the same, utterly enlightened, and most rare position as that of the biblical prophet. It is a terrible tension to hold, but also a terribly creative tension for history.

Isaiah, it seems, must create the dissonance and the conflict to preserve the soul of the nation. He is not finally concerned about politics, because it will all pass away anyway. He is concerned about using historical events to transform consciousness, and to do this he must point out that "the heart of this people is gross, its ears dull." He needs to create moral dilemmas for people, to trap them in their confusion, so that they can face their shadow self, own their biases and loyalties, and possibly come to consciousness. Yahweh, for Isaiah, is "sanctuary and stumbling stone, the rock that brings us down, a trap and a snare" (8:14), for both the heart and the soul. I understand this only because I see it happen now and then at retreats and conferences. The very ones who hate and fight you the most are often the ones who fall into grace most dramatically by the end. Most of us seem to think that our job is to answer people's questions and take away their anxiety. Not so with Isaiah. He creates new and deeper questions of conscience and integrity for Israel. He allows God to "leave towns deserted" and "houses untenanted" and to "create a great emptiness in the country" (6:11). What perfect metaphors for the creating of liminal space, where, I believe, all true transformation happens.

It seems that the prophet's job is first to deconstruct current illusions, which is the status quo, and then reconstruct on a new and honest foundation. That is why the prophet is never popular with the comfortable or with those in power. Few except the "holy seed" have any patience with the deconstruction of egos and institutions.

The prophet leads us through "the way of the fall," whereas the job of the priest is to lead us onto the "way of the return." What we have most of the time is lots of priests and almost no prophets. We priests glibly talk about the great kingdom of God or the coming of Jesus at Christmas, but we do not take the time to detach people from their smaller kingdoms and loyalties to make that coming possible. As a result, very little new happens, and the day after Christmas is pretty much like the day before. The prophets, instead, are "radical" teachers in the truest sense of the word; they go to the root causes and root vices and "root" them out! Their educational method is to expose and accuse with no holds barred. Ministers and religion in general tend to concentrate on effects and symptoms, usually a mopping up exercise after the fact. As someone once put it, we throw life preservers to people drowning in the swollen stream, which is all well and good; but prophets work way upstream to find out why the stream is swollen in the first place.

Faith, for Isaiah, is not believing in doctrines, finding security in institutions, or belonging to groups (because he has deconstructed all of these), but *an active and positive accepting of what is*—moment by moment, event by event, tragedy by tragedy, grace by grace. Faith allowed Isaiah not only to see God in all things but to believe that God could and would use all things for God's purposes in history. We join Isaiah when we also see the "glory that fills the whole earth"—which is always hidden amid the "smoke filling the temple" and by the "seraph wings" that cover the Holy Presence (6:2-5). It is a seeing that is taught, given, and allowed by God.

That sounds like unhealthy fatalism to the dualistic mind, as it did to the pragmatics of Isaiah's own day, but that is to sell biblical faith far too short. Let God "shut your eyes so that you will not see with your eyes," and then allow you "to see and see again" (6:9), and then you can know for yourself what Isaiah already knows,

> Your salvation lies in complete surrender and tranquility,
> your strength lies in complete trust. (30:15)

And that is being spoken when the Egyptians are beating down the door, and when the king has every good reason to form alliances with just about anybody! But remember, Isaiah is not concerned about political or social expediency; he is concerned about the soul of the nation and about forcing ultimate questions upon them. History, for this man, is merely a staging ground for God.

John the Baptist

The First Necessary Freedom

A man came from God. His name was John. He came as a witness, as a witness to speak for the light, so that everyone might believe through him. He was not the light, only a witness to speak for the light.

John 1:6-8

A voice cries, "Prepare in the wilderness a path for the Lord, make a straight highway for our God across the desert. Let every valley be filled in, every mountain and hill be laid low, let every cliff become a plain, and the ridges a valley. And the glory of God shall be revealed, and all humankind shall see it, for the mouth of Yahweh has spoken."

Isaiah 40:3-5

This man wore a garment made of camel hair with a leather belt around his waist, and his food was locusts and wild honey. . . . He said, "I baptize with water, but there is one coming after me who baptizes with the Holy Spirit and fire."

Matthew 3:4, 11

This complex man needs three different passages from the Bible to set his big stage. He has always been a favorite of mine, but, like so many of the others, he has been too "churchified" and has lost most of his power and message. I have always felt that he would not be allowed in any self-respecting Christian sanctuary (even those named after him and with golden statues of him). He would surely not be admitted to a seminary or even a lay ministry program (poor social skills and serious dress code violations), and he would never be canonized by the recent Roman processes (too critical of the church establishment down at the temple, taking away their business besides). Yet he is the one of whom Jesus says, "I tell you solemnly, of all the children born of women, a greater than John the Baptist has never been seen!" (Matthew 11:11). Wow! That is no faint praise. Why does he merit this accolade?

Let's start with those texts from Scripture. I take the Prologue to the Gospel of John first, because it states without apology that "he was not the light, but only a witness to" it. This is straightforward indeed, because I don't think John the Baptist is that much of a light at all, especially in relation to the grace, freedom, breadth, and depth that we soon see in Jesus. He is Jesus' "country cousin," who gets the ball rolling and fortunately gets out of the way quickly. For that Jesus—and I—are very grateful. Jesus' praise is sincere, because John did his job of linking the old with the new, and that is quite a task. But once the linkage and pointing forward are finished, John rightly leaves the stage and, as we know, does it most graciously with a little help from Salome and her platter.

The second passage is from the initiatory call of Second Isaiah, which is quoted in each of the Synoptic Gospels, but in part or even incorrectly. I thought it would be helpful to get back to the source that first inspired the evangelists and made them see John the Baptist as its fulfillment. This passage outlines Isaiah's own vocation as one who is to make God more easily accessible to *"all* the peoples," but especially for the deportees in Babylon as they return home. The images are unforgettable and dramatic. Mountains clearly refer to the arrogance of the powerful (see 2:14); the valleys are all those obstacle courses and potholes that debt and purity codes have put in the way, and the words "all" and "every" are not to be tripped over lightly. There is clearly a new universalism in Second Isaiah, who has been humbled and purified during his (or probably her!) time in exile. But what we have here is a new exodus, a new march out of an ever new slavery, and Isaiah's job is to facilitate it and open it up. To see John the Baptist as this builder of a superhighway is real genius on the part of the evangelists, and he seems to have served precisely that function in the historical situation. He might be moralistic and harsh, but at least he is emphasizing real social evils and not just offenses against the purity system or the liturgical debt codes (Luke 3:10-14).

John the Baptizer, whether he was a part of the community of the Dead Sea Scrolls or not, clearly represented a break from temple-controlled religion. In the face of all the debt codes and purity codes and animal sacrifices, there was this upstart outsider going down to the river and proclaiming the forgiveness of sins—and calling them a "brood of vipers" besides! This is no way to establish a proper ecumenical dialogue. It is no surprise that the Jerusalem establishment sent a quick delegation to check out his credentials and his orthodoxy (see John 1:19-25). John's popularity was so great that they dared not oppose him, which says a lot in itself about their supposed concern about orthodoxy (John 3:22-27). The trouble is that John was the son of a priestly family; Zechariah and Elizabeth both had impressive résumés (Luke 1:5), but their son clearly did not live up to them. One can only hope that John's father was long gone and did not have to face the priestly club on the golf course. His son was surely a scandal, a disappointment, and in camel hair besides! Not to speak of his strange vegetarian diet.

Which leads us to the third reading. The depiction of John the Baptist seems to go to great lengths to show that this man was not representing church business as usual! It is quite clear in the law how sin is to be forgiven, and the scribes are those who broker that forgiveness by the official "confessional practice": admission of sin, firm purpose of amendment, and appropriate penance—animal sacrifice or tithe afterward. How dare this son of a priest make God's forgiveness as available as water in the river! Remember, John's baptism was always announced as "for the forgiveness of sin" (Mark 1:5; Matthew 3:6; Luke 3:3). This is why it is so shocking to Christians that Jesus even submitted to it. You see why I said that John is a complex and even scary figure, and why we had to domesticate him. As even the costume, location, and non-kosher diet make clear, this baptizer is not a company man. Yet that is what we have made him into— leading to nice christening ceremonies in white lace dresses. In time his job description became the one who points to and proves that our God is best, instead of one who *lives* a radical critique of religion, morality, and priesthood itself.

After saying all of that, I now want to counter it by saying also that I think John the Baptist is only a *first-stage-of-life*

prophet. He had the freedom, the passion, and the clear boundaries that are needed to get *anything* started. But Jesus goes on to say, after praising him so profusely, that the very least in his "kingdom of God" is greater than John the Baptist! (Matthew 11:11). Yes, John is a wild man who "clears the threshing floor," but after that he really does not have much to do. It takes a *second-stage-of-life man* like Jesus to know how to make food out of the seed that has been winnowed, and how to heal and use the chaff that John has no patience with (Matthew 3:12). I love John as far as he goes, but perhaps the reason that we continue to keep him as a totem is that much of Christianity is still the religion of John the Baptist and not of Jesus. John was being absolutely honest when he said to Jesus, "It is I who need baptism from you (John 3:13). Mine is merely a water ritual . . . but what you are talking about is the real transformation of persons by Spirit and fire" (Matthew 3:11). Yet how much of Christian history has been arguing about the when, who, how, and where of the mere water ritual! When is it valid or licit? Does our denomination honor your water ritual? And so on. Yes, we are the moralistic and ritualistic religion of John the Baptist for the most part, after he himself said, "I am not the one!" I am not the Christ, I am not Elijah, and I am not the prophet, he shouts (John 1:21-23). I am just a voice yelling into the wind. Just as when people say, "You might as well be talking to a door," John goes outside the city and the temple and "cries out in the wilderness." They can't hear him in the city center.

What makes this man extraordinary is not his teaching. He is a narrow and righteous moralist. He has not passed over to the second half of life yet. He has not "died." He would never heal or reconcile anything. What makes him great is not his manner. He is needlessly abrasive and enjoys being an opponent and even grandstanding. What makes John "the greatest" is his modest and realistic knowledge of who he is in the great drama of salvation, when he clearly is drawing big crowds and could form his own denomination or mega-church on the south side of Jerusalem. Men such as John are most rare. They are witnesses to the truth, pointing beyond themselves and getting out of the way so that the true light can shine through. John is the first necessary freedom that gets everything started: freedom *from* himself and therefore freedom *for* a bigger message.

This is what Jesus loved about his cousin, John, and why we could and should love him ourselves. He is excellent in his job and absolutely needed as far as he goes. But we are not "Baptists"; we are finally and hopefully Christians.

$\mathcal{P}$eter

He Came to God by Doing It Wrong

Simon Peter said, "I'm going fishing." The other disciples replied, "We'll come with you." They went out and got into the boat and caught nothing that night.

It was light by now, and there stood Jesus on the shore, though the disciples did not realize that it was Jesus. . . . [Eventually] the disciple whom Jesus loved said to Peter, "It is the Lord!" At these words, "It is the Lord," Simon Peter, who had practically nothing on, wrapped his cloak around him and jumped into the water. The other disciples came on in the boat, towing the net and the fish [that they had just caught by following Jesus' advice]; they were only about a hundred yards from land.

As soon as they came ashore they saw that there was some bread there, and a charcoal fire with fish cooking on it.

John 21:3-4, 7-9

Why was this man given any keys? There they are, so clearly at the bottom of the portrait and emblazoned all over Rome too. Why would this largely unsuccessful working man be given the keys to anything? I remember my first visit to St. Peter's in Rome, standing in awe at the back entrance trying to take it all in, when a poorly dressed old man took his place at my side, mumbled a few words in Italian, and quickly walked back out. I asked my friar partner, who spoke Italian, what he had said. Laughing out loud, he told me that the old man had muttered in disgust "pretty nice tomb for a fisherman!" He was probably one of those Italian communists.

This whole Gospel story, with its cast of constantly unlikely and unpious people, reaches the level of farce when we come to Peter. He is the only one whom Jesus ever calls a devil (Mark 8:33); he is the only one who directly denies Jesus (Mark 14:66-72); his first response in every encounter is always wrong; and yet he is clearly the one whom Jesus makes the spokesman and the symbol for this whole new enterprise that he is starting. Now what is going on here? I think it is something very good indeed, when the one "with practically nothing on" can become the leader.

Peter is undoubtedly everyman and everywoman. Peter is humanity at its most lovable, disheartening best. Peter has a working-class, uneducated man's response to life. He does not filter things through his head, like people who write books such as this. He filters it through an immediate instinctive response, which is not to filter it at all. What else would a passage communicate, or be trying to communicate, which has the poor guy put *on* his clothes before he jumps into the water, while the rest take the reasonable one-hundred-yard boat ride to shore? Are these asides merely accidental, or are they trying to tell us the very character and temperament of this most central Gospel figure? Peter is often presented as a bit of a buffoon—but the very buffoon that we all are and that God in Jesus loves and uses for God's purposes.

What a shame that we have taken this immensely hopeful symbol of us all and dressed him up in tiara and tinsel. What a tragedy for history that what should be his inherent power has been a source of argument, division, and assertion, instead of a power for human and social transformation. The Dalai Lama has a freedom that popes can only long for. Jesus gave Peter to us to affirm our obvious fallibility and our very usable failures, and we turned him around and made him "infallible"—the one thing that his life never exemplifies or illustrates. It is so self-evidently contrary to the text that for me it illustrates the old axiom, "If you want to tell a lie and get away with it, tell a really big one." Most people do not have the courage to think you could be that wrong; however, the Scriptures do.

But who is the villain here? Or do we even need a villain? I am convinced that it is not some nefarious lot in Rome seeking power. It is much more the very natural worldview of those who already have power. When you look at life from the top, which we pretty much have since the Constantinian revolution, you cannot read texts in light of change and transformation; you read them in terms of self-maintenance and the status quo. This is not malicious; it is just predictable and somewhat blind. Peter the failing fisherman "who catches nothing all night" is largely a judgment on history and our infatuation with power and office. He is a critique of our level of human development up to now, but also a lure to call us farther. Maybe this is why God needed Peter to be a fisherman. A fisherman knows the power of bait, and he knows the patience of waiting. Peter is indeed "a fisher of men," a lure for humanity, even if we have seldom allowed ourselves to be caught by his torn net.

Jesus foresees all of this coming when he talks to Peter and the disciples at the Last Supper itself. They are again arguing about who is the greatest. Jesus says that this is "the way it is among pagans," but "this is not to happen among you. No, the greatest among you must behave as if he were the least, the leader as one who serves" (Luke 22:25-26). Servant leadership, the authority that comes from being at the bottom, is the authority that finally convinces and converts people. It is based not on *potestas*, the power to enforce, but on *auctoritas*, the power of inherent truth. One sees it in people like Nelson Mandela, Mother Teresa, and Mahatma Gandhi. They have the authority that comes from lifestyle, and they do not need any throne or special hat to assert it. Thank God, Pope Paul VI got rid of the tiara, the ermine trains, and the carried throne, which the medievals probably needed. Or did they?

Knowing this message will be very hard for the disciples to understand, Jesus enacts the role of servant authority himself (22:27), hoping that the image will be imprinted in their memory. The honest remembrance of Scripture is always a "dangerous memory" for power and pretense.

On the personal level, which is where it all starts, Peter is a grand and honest statement about how we all come to God. This pattern is a great surprise, and for many a great shock and even a disappointment. We clearly come to God not by doing it right but ironically by doing it wrong. This message is very clear in almost every biblical character, with the possible exception of Mary. Not one of them would have been canonized by the later criteria of holiness. Biblical holiness has to do with God's call, grace, and faithfulness to us, and not the faithfulness of our response, which is why the text goes out of its way to show Peter's first response as almost always incorrect, and his second response almost always forced upon him by the goodness and patience of Jesus. Check it out for yourself in all of the Peter stories. He is the first in foolishness, and the first in surrender. That is the normal path. Until the cock crows, we do not get it. Until the cock crows, we do not see God. Until the cock crows, we do not know ourselves. We are all saved in spite of ourselves, and never is that more clearly illustrated than in the life of Peter. God does not love Peter because Peter is good. God loves Peter because God is good, and that is what Peter finally sees and what makes him fall in love with Jesus in return. Finally, Peter the everyman runs with John the beloved to the resurrection, always trying to catch up.

We see it all in the lovely account of John 20:1-10. They are both presented in perfect archetypal symmetry: John is "love" (20:2), which always gets to the truth first and more quickly, yet enters in humbly after Peter, and immediately "believes." Peter, the community and the everyman that "follow," enters rashly with no mention of belief or encounter, and then goes "home again" (20:10). It is not that one is right and the other wrong, because we know they both eventually encountered and believed. It is a question of both-and; it is a question of timing and temperament. Love is always the surer path to life, the quicker way to move beyond crucifixion. But *faith community is the path that keeps us in the arena of love for the long struggle.* John recognizes this and defers to Peter and lets him enter first. I had the container much earlier than I discovered its real contents.

The Gospel keeps us in the full tension between container and contents, medium and message, wineskins and wine. Peter is the container, which is usually slow, brittle, and even boring; John is the contents, which is new wine and thrilling message. But Jesus is realistic enough to know that "new wine must be put into new wineskins—so that *both* can be preserved" (Matthew 9:17)! It will never be a really popular message, especially in these days of intense individualism and fast food. We would sooner just buy our wine at the drive-up liquor window and take off.

I know myself that I could never say the things I am writing in this book, if I had not been carried and sustained by the boat of Peter over the big lake of my life. It is the church itself that has empowered me and even compels me to criticize the church. It is the Gospel that this community proclaims that has taught me the values and criteria by which I judge that very community. It is Peter's message that has held me long enough so that I could recognize John's message. Once I knew that fallible, failing men like Peter were the norm, then I was able to hope for love—and found hope for myself.

The tiredness that we see on Peter's face is the tiredness both of being shamelessly used by those in power and of being arrogantly ignored by those who will not stay with him at the oars of the boat.

$\mathcal{P}$aul

A Man of Contradictions

It was to shame the wise that God chose what is foolish by human reckoning, and to shame what is strong that he chose what is weak by human reckoning; those whom the world thinks common and contemptible are the ones that God has chosen—those who are nothing at all to show up those who are everything. The human race has nothing to boast about to God.

1 Corinthians 1:28-30

What eyes! What is it that Paul looks at so intently? What is the surrounding darkness that he looks out from? Then we look back at him with awe and admiration, and a bit of mistrust—at this Jewish man who is rightly considered one of the ten most influential men in human history. There is a disturbed and anxious look in his eyes. Is he looking outside or inside? Or is he making the connection between the two? I believe that was much of his genius and his conflict.

Did Saul really die when Paul was born on that road to Damascus? Or was Saul always in the background, the raw material of God's new creation? Was Saul really a bad man, the righteous ideologue that we all love to hate? Or was Paul such a good man since most find him hard to love? Perhaps you see where I am going with this.

For the rest of his life and in all of his letters, Paul seems to love and understand paradox. He prefers the "dialectical method," and he teaches through contrast, comparison, and the overcoming of seeming contradictions. Those who read him superficially have almost always made one of the sides bad and the other good, for example, flesh and spirit, but this is largely to miss his genius as a teacher. If one has not consciously struggled, and partly reconciled, these patterns inside of oneself, I think it is almost impossible to understand the great St. Paul. Like Socrates and all wisdom teachers, he is a midwife and can bring out only what is already there. I myself, for example, have found that one is largely wasting one's time talking about "contemplation" to a person who has not had at least one moment of undeserved and unexpected communion.

Yes, you can choose to resent and reject Paul for many understandable reasons, but know that you are missing an opportunity to leap into the fray of full humanness. He, like the Scriptures themselves, is a "text in travail," to use René Girard's wonderfully illuminating phrase. He gives you some answers, yes, but only by allowing you first of all to experience the dilemma and the struggle within yourself. He *is* the problem personified. He *is* the human paradox and the human possibility. Stay with him, and you will see your own life caught up in the same text and the same travail.

All humans are filled with contradictions, waiting to be reconciled. Just one of Paul's numerous leaps into these contradictions is enough to make him a genius, a mystic, and a first-rate seer. We see one of his resolutions in the topsy-turvy quotation that begins this meditation. What is wisdom and what is foolishness after reading such a passage? Paul leads you into liminal space—and leaves you there for a while—until you grow up a little more. And he even dared to write in such a way to the ordered and Apollonian Greek mind, which needed and demanded resolution. The man is either very wise or very foolish himself. It is this seeming paradox that he has overcome within himself and then courageously asserts. Although he would be the first to say that he did not overcome it, he *was overcome*. He likes the words "captured" or "grasped" to communicate the experience (Philippians 3:13).

The "language of the cross" (1 Corinthians 1:18) became for Paul a different "philosopher's stone," his own template by which to evaluate and critique the meaning of reality. It allowed him to break through what seemed like order and logic to discover a new order, which he called "the hidden wisdom of God." It could never be arrived at by mere study or intelligence, but only by *surrender to communion,* which he called faith. He used a juridical word, "justification," to describe that reunion. Now we might speak of ultimate validation, mirroring, or "salvation." But Paul knew that the only way this realignment would take place was through an ego-stripping experience that tore away our false and fabricated self and led us into a new self (Ephesians 2:15 or Galatians 6:15), where all the contradictions could be absorbed and overcome. It had happened in him, and now he saw his life as "handing on this reconciliation" (2 Corinthians 5:18), which was always through the coincidence of opposites, called the cross.

The cross, even geometrically, is a collision of two opposing lines. Paul knew by his unwarranted election that God had not eliminated or expelled his former self, but instead had "incorporated" it into the Christ Self. He knew that he was still a mass of contradictions and inconsistencies, which is exactly what is written all over the pages of his letters. Yet his absolute confidence was not in his personal wholeness, but in the one who had grafted him into the Wholeness of

God, Jesus. This is the total basis of his joy, his love, his daring self-confidence, and his impassioned desire to have everyone else experience the same transformation and this same ecstasy.

Let's just list the seeming dualisms that Paul loves to play with and try to reconcile: law and spirit, flesh and Spirit, the old self and the new self, Adam and Christ, weakness and strength, foolishness and wisdom, Jew and Gentile, election by race and election by grace, works and mercy, exclusivity and inclusivity, law and freedom, worthiness and chosenness, individuation and community, the perfection that comes from obedience and the perfection that comes from surrender, office and charism, the twelve apostles and his own apostleship. In each case, he is describing something that has already been overcome in him through his life conflicts; thus he does not see them as opposites, even though he still "suffers" them as inner conflicts (see, for example, Romans 7:14-25). For Paul, Christ is the one who overcomes all of these opposites in him and Christ is the one who holds his disparate parts together in the mercy that he first met on the Damascus road. How could he not be passionately in love with such a Christ, even if he remained a Jew till the end?

In each case there is a tension between what seems like a pattern or structure and God's freedom to break the pattern and introduce anti-structure. Stay with Paul long enough, and you will always see this tension, even though individual passages might look like pure structure and others look like pure anti-structure. Remember, he himself is a text in travail, just as we are. It is a Greater Love that holds it all together in him. It is a Larger Love that has captured him.

It is almost as if human consciousness was not ready to see this creative tension up to now. Most of the quoting of Paul's letters in church has been on the side of structure, and we have been blind and unwilling to see his clearly anti-structure opinions, many of which are quite iconoclastic and dangerous to a religion that is primarily trying to create order in a disordered world. But neither Jesus nor Paul is especially concerned about order, niceness, or social control. They are concerned about transformation of persons and history, and about using the very disorder of people's lives to bring them to God. That is why it is called good news by both of them, and why it is a surprising and joyful discovery for anyone who is honest about their state. What we largely have in Western religion today is bad news. It is an attempt to super-impose an impossible order on a world that God allows to be disordered, and in which God even uses the disorder to bring us all to Love. How could we miss or avoid such utter good news?

It is this anguish that I see in the eyes of Paul, but it is this solution that drives him on without flagging. He wants all to *enjoy* this same favor. "Yes, we are weak, as he [Jesus] was, but we shall live with him through the power of God, for your benefit" (2 Corinthians 13:4). Paul knows where his strength lies and he knows where his wound is, but his spiritual genius is that he has connected the two! Most of Christian history has tried to disconnect the two, and the results have been disguise, denial, and boredom with an unworkable message. Paul's theology of "earthenware jars" (2 Corinthians 4:7) and "thorns that keep me from getting too proud"

(2 Corinthians 12:7) becomes the mind-boggling but utterly hopeful spirituality of vulnerability or "imperfection," which has been no more than a subtext in most of Jewish and Christian history. We don't like vulnerability very much, even though we are the only religion that literally worships a graphically wounded man.

It started with God saying to Israel that their election was precisely because they were "the least" of all the peoples (Deuteronomy 7:7), through the almost embarrassing usage of barren women, forgotten sons, obvious sinners, and handicapped people, to Jesus' shocking opener, "Blessed are the poor in spirit." It reappears in the desert fathers and mothers, in Francis of Assisi, Vincent de Paul, Thérèse of Lisieux, and Dorothy Day, and shows itself today in the spirituality of Alcoholics Anonymous.

But the primary text in history has always been the ego's agenda of "onward and upward," ascent rather than descent, spiritual imperialism (which was then replicated in society). A "spirituality of perfection" is a divine or maybe mathematical concept and not a human one at all. Paul was, instead, the theoretician of the scandal that had happened in the life and death of Jesus, but most of Christian history has been unable to carry this "sign of contradiction" (Luke 2:34). Ideas of winning and losing, success, reward, punishment, sacrifice, and worthiness seem to be hard-wired into our psyches. Grace has never come easily. For some reason, the ego mistrusts anything that is free. It fears anything that names our littleness instead of our bigness, our needy desire instead of our heroic devotion.

Now look again and through those clear, hopeful, but anguished eyes of Paul. Note the sword of the word of God that stands in front of him. Like few in history, he has grabbed that physician's scalpel, "which is something alive and active, cutting like any double-edged sword, but more finely yet. It slips through the place where soul is divided from spirit, joints from marrow. It judges secret emotions and thoughts . . . before it, everything is uncovered and open" (Hebrews 4:12-13). Let him do his surgery on you. It is major surgery, but the results are also major.

They say that Paul was killed by a sword. I wonder if they are not the same sword. The message that leaves us uncovered and open to God is the very same message that leaves us naked to our enemies. Perhaps that is why history has always been afraid of Paul's sword.

$\mathcal{T}$imothy

A Beginner's Mind

Do not let people disregard you because you are young, but be an example to all the believers in the way you speak and behave, and in your love, your faith, and your purity. Make use of the time until I arrive by reading to the people, preaching, and teaching. You have in you a spiritual gift which was given to you when the prophets spoke and the body of elders laid their hands on you; do not let it lie unused. . . . Do not speak harshly to a man older than yourself, but advise him as you would your own father; treat the younger men as brothers, and older women as you would your mother. Always treat younger women with propriety, as if they were your sisters. . . . And you should give up drinking only water and have a little wine for the sake of your digestion and the frequent bouts of illness that you have.

I Timothy 4:12–5:2, 23

Do you see that receptive look on Tim's face? I wonder where it comes from. Is it humility? Is it groundedness? Or is it just fear? Was he just smart enough to defer to the obvious greatness of Paul and Jesus? Or was he just a fearful follower. The letters of Paul give a very positive impression of Timothy as a man who could be taught to be a leader. What gave him such a teachable spirit so young? Why was Paul able to form him so early in his life? My own experience of working with men today is that unless you have power over them by reason of salary, office, or law, they are not very accountable, much less teachable. What happened here with this young disciple Timothy that made him so different? If Paul is the classic mentor, I guess we would have to say that Timothy is the classic "mentee."

I know the name is a derivative of the word for "fear," and maybe Timothy was just afraid of being wrong or afraid of not being liked or just afraid of himself, as many of us are. If that is true, he made a virtue out of it. His fear was seemingly transmuted into what we call "beginner's mind," which is what grace always does—it turn our vices into another way to love and serve God's reality. What starts as timidity becomes humility and openness and teachability. Bad self-doubt becomes the healthy self-reflection that you wish more men had! It is that enduring sense of openness and humility that does not close down by reason of failure, facts, or cynical old age. It asks for and listens to good advice. It creates and values team over grandstanding and self-made careers. Not much admired in America today, in fact, it is even devalued in our elected leaders.

Timothy's timidity has been turned into true courage and healthy loyalty. Now he becomes Paul's constant traveling companion all over Asia Minor and Macedonia; he submits to circumcision as an adult (which we men know is not something we would eagerly await!); he is sent ahead on his own, left behind by himself, allowed to be his own man while still young, commissioned by Paul to discern, appoint, and reprimand elders—and all in cultures that honored only age, rank, and title. He had none of these, but only a passion and dedication that made Paul call him "my brother," "God's helper," "my dear and faithful son," and "true child in the faith." Timothy's awareness of his own limitations has become loyalty to the limitlessness of God and loyalty to Paul his teacher, who must have dazzled him with his daring and his iconoclasm. Timothy's intense knowledge that *he* cannot do it gives him the certainty that God *is* doing it. His healthy self-doubt allows him to trust and admire another. Not a bad metamorphosis for fear.

It seems that our vices do not just go away; they are used to heal us by a very enterprising God, like the serpent that first bit the Israelites in the desert (Numbers 21:9). Today we call it homeopathic medicine, and we see the serpent symbol on the physician's logo. God uses everything we do, even our mistakes, to bring us to our own Godself. The divine economy is, indeed, very "economical." God includes the failure to create the victory—which is the ultimate way to create victory. The true win/win situation. The mistakes and the limitations are still there, but they have become refined into a gift that we can hardly take credit for ourselves. As C. G. Jung was fond of saying, "Where we stumble and fall, there we find pure gold." All that we can personally take credit for is the fall, not the rising. It is a sign of true enlightenment to know that to be true.

Thus the common cliché from the saints that used to seem so disingenuous, "I am only responsible for my sins, but my goodness is totally from God." Objectively they are correct. Timothy, like anyone who has ever lived honestly or humbly, knows that this is not a cliché but a certainty.

~

There could be another possibility too. The fear that the name Timothy points to could also be translated "awe-filled" or "wonderstruck" or "enthrallment." We see it in almost all descriptions of authentic religious encounter. Every biblical theophany from Moses to Mary speaks of the recipient as being "afraid" in this sense, and yet the word from God is invariably the opposite: "Do not be afraid." The only appropriate response to the Infinite would surely be an overwhelming sense of our own finiteness and incapacity to receive. Yet God invites us in anyway. "Don't waste time asking questions of worthiness," God seems to say. "I am not concerned about worthiness but about readiness and receptivity." To be wonderstruck is to allow the distinction, to suffer one's own littleness and to stand under the mercy anyway. "He looks upon me *in my lowliness,* and all generations shall call me blessed," Mary says (Luke 1:48). These are the chosen, who are never the same as the worthy. Yes, many are called, in fact all. But very few allow themselves to be chosen (Matthew 22:14). They would rather be "worthy."

I think there are some hints that this might indeed be the case with little Timothy here, looking at us so humbly with his clear brown eyes. He appears not self-defeated but utterly centered. He holds the mystery inside and behind those gently folded hands. He is surely in awe of something, but utterly content, and for the right reason he appears even self-sufficient. Have you ever met a man like that? I have. Their inner enthrallment enthralls you too. They seem dazzled by something very real, and it bedazzles you just to be around them. I think Jesus had that effect on Paul, Paul had it on Timothy, and now Timothy on us. I think it is the real and final meaning of apostolic succession. Not so much a laying on of hands as a passing on of energy and life.

There are a few lines in Paul's letters that suggest that Timothy was, indeed, an "enthralled" man. (This is all we can rely on, since we have no record of Tim's own sermons or writings. Even in this, he seems to have been self-effacing with no need to be public or published.) First of all, there is no record of any marriage or children, but instead he seems to have an overwhelming sense of a personal call. In Paul's words, Timothy has made "the preaching of the Good News his life's work, in thoroughgoing service" (2 Timothy 4:5). He also says of Timothy, "you spoke up for the truth in front of many witnesses" (1 Timothy 6:12). Then he adds, "Always I remember you in my prayers, and I remember your tears, and I long to see you again to complete my happiness. And I am aware of the sincere faith which you have" (2 Timothy 1:3-4). Finally he ends his second letter begging Timothy three times to come and visit him! There is no other relationship like this in all of Paul's letters.

Obviously, he was a joy, a son, and a personal strength to the great Paul, who otherwise appeared to need no one. I know, as a teacher and preacher myself, what a deep consolation it is to have one person who fully and authentically has absorbed your message. It is the reality check that you yourself need to be assured that your intangible message has at least some tangibility, and that you are not crazy. Timothy, I believe, was Paul's trainee and alter ego, along with being a "true child of mine" to a man who had no children of his own. Spiritual generation can be even more powerful than physical, and Paul refers to this proudly several times (1 Thessalonians 2:11-12; 1 Corinthians 4:15; Philemon 10). Paul clearly has a very strong paternal instinct, and here we see his transmutation from something merely physical to something very generative for the masses.

His highly personal ("have some wine for your digestion") and fatherly ("remember who your teacher was") mentoring of Timothy was a two-way street. Like the Trinity itself, which Paul was beginning to intuit: the Father needs to give himself totally to another to experience his own Life as his own, and the Son needs to be totally given to by another to know that what he thinks is his own life is not his at all. It is the oldest pattern of the universe—written into physics, biology, psychology, and every sexual encounter. Who is doing the giving and who is doing the receiving almost has no answer. All we know is that we do not hold our lives autonomously. Neither did Paul. Neither did Timothy. And neither did Jesus. They all received their lives as gifts and gave them back in the same manner. Such men are truly "sons," always receiving, always in awe, always beginning anew to recognize the mystery that is endless and bottomless.

———

The reason that Timothy and Paul have come down to us in history is that they were somehow open *to* and in awe *of* this exchange, to which they were only but always witnesses. They must have known deeply that they were being used. They were instruments of a much larger exchange, about which they could only stutter and stammer. They called it "preaching the gospel," which was a new phrase altogether, although it has now been trivialized by too-glib repetition.

Timothy had that enduring and rare beginner's mind, and maybe it was even his weakness or vice, but in a certain sense he gave it back as a virtue to the overly self-assured Paul, who finally learned that "it was when he was weak that he was strong" (2 Corinthians 12:10). This ever-rediscovered beginner's mind, which is a deathlike vulnerability before reality, kept each of them forever growing and forever young. They kept each other in contact with a pattern that was very old and endlessly fruitful—the vulnerable pattern of the universe, which is always, it seems, beginning anew.

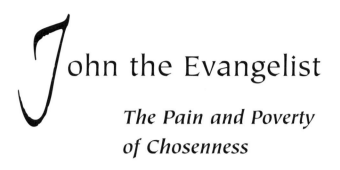

John the Evangelist

The Pain and Poverty
of Chosenness

Peter turned and saw the disciple Jesus loved following them—the one who had leaned on his breast at the supper and had said to him, "Lord, who is it that will betray you?"

Seeing him, Peter said to Jesus, "What about him, Lord?"

Jesus answered, "If I want him to stay behind till I come, what does it matter to you? Your job is to follow me."

The rumor then went out among the brothers that this disciple would not die. Yet Jesus had not said to Peter, "He will not die," but "If I want him to stay behind until I come, what is that to you?"

John 21:20-23

Wow! There is a lot written between the lines here, as there surely is in all multi-layered sacred texts. There is a very human dynamic at work between Peter and John in these lines and a very human warning for almost all of us who are like them.

Frankly, I smell envy, even in the prince of the apostles, who had just been the center of attention in the previous episode. Males do not surrender their grandiosity easily. Jesus has just told Peter about "being led where he would rather not go" (21:18), and we immediately see him unwilling to do just that. He is quickly trying to control and maybe even compete with "the beloved disciple." The Gospels are not afraid to present the prototypical believer, Peter, as a slow learner. Obviously, this gives hope and confidence to all the rest of us. Jesus is clearly telling Peter to mind his own business and to put his attention on his own difficult task ahead of him, but Peter is seemingly threatened by the favored position of John, even though he has plenty of favor himself. He is oh so human, thank God, with little hint of infallibility yet.

Just a moment before, Peter had had the Master's eye, and he looked around to see the one who is invariably running ahead of him physically (see John 20:4), but maybe in spiritual insight and in favor too. He is stung by those old demons of comparison and competition. Like a jealous schoolboy, he asks, "You tell me I am going to have to suffer! What about him? Is he going to have to suffer too? Or does he just have to lay his head on your breast? It feels to me that you are predicting death for me, but eternal life for him! I don't like this very much. In fact, I don't like *him!*" Who of us cannot see ourselves in this rapidly advancing scenario of hurt feelings, projections, and judgments? It says much more about Peter than it does about John, but let's look at John for now.

Study the face in Louis Glanzman's marvelous portrait. Do you see what I see? An eager and virile young man, filled with energy for life and task, in fact already carrying his product and his success in his one hand. The other hand is free for even more, clenched in conviction and desire. But look again. Is that anguish? Or is it confusion? Or doubt? John is already paying the price, even among the other chosen, for being "more chosen"! Yes, he is the archetype of the mystic lover, the one who gets to everything first and faster (John 20:5), but he also pays the price that mystics often do, even from the church itself—if we are to see Peter as the archetype of the church, which is what Catholic tradition has always taught. To put it another way, institution always fears and mistrusts charism. There is a tension between priests and mystics, between those who represent order and those who represent passion. It is a necessary but ongoing and very real tension in the life of all spiritual groups. Often it is never resolved and leads to accusation or even schism. "Mystics" have to keep careful watch over their grandiosity. True religious encounter is always dangerous for the ego, precisely because it is so magnificent.

John's greatest persecution might well have come from the community of believers itself rather than from any outside unbelievers or authorities. In fact, studies of the Letters of

John seem to indicate that this was precisely the case (see Raymond E. Brown, *The Community of the Beloved Disciple* [New York: Paulist Press, 1979]). But is that not true of most of us? It is our own families, friends, and home communities that try us and test us the most. As Jesus predicted, "A man's enemies will be those of his own household" (Matthew 10:36). Or, as the Psalmist puts it, "If an enemy had done this, I could have understood it, but you, you my own brother, who walked with me in the house of God!" Civil wars are the most violent, I hear, because the ones closest to us are the greatest threat and carry our most fearful projections. Priests and mystics are probably a necessary foil for one another. Priests tend to carry the short sprint, but mystics always win the marathon.

John is not only the archetype of the mystic, the lover, the chosen son; he is also the bearer of the *agony* of all chosenness. Election is seldom appreciated by others; it is seldom honored as a true touch from God. Our personal insecurity and neediness are too great to recognize and delight in the specialness of anyone else. Others are a threat to our zero-sum existence. Beloved status is almost always mistrusted, envied, judged, and even persecuted. That is the burden of being a chosen son or daughter. Read the lives of saints and religious founders. Most of their persecution comes from their own families, and very often from church authorities. In the book of Jonah, it is the good and pious men who throw Jonah overboard (1:14-16), while covering their attempted homicide with prayer, God-talk, and the making of heroic vows.

We see the exact same pattern in the life of Joseph and his brothers (Genesis 37:4): "His brothers, seeing how his father loved him more than all his other sons, came to hate him so much that they could not say a civil word to him." Eventually they threw him into the mythic pit, decided to kill him, and finally settled on selling him into slavery to save their own honor. But God's election will not be stopped. We know that Joseph comes back to save these very brothers, almost like Nelson Mandela inviting his jailers to his inauguration party of the new South Africa. In fact, I would say that beloved status is proved precisely by the freedom to recognize and delight in beloved status in others! Chosen people show that they are truly chosen by extending that same experience of chosenness to others. In fact, I would take that as the test of true election. When certain denominations cannot see "savedness" outside their own group, it is a sure sign that they themselves are not saved by any salvation worth the name. John spends the rest of his life creating a community and a Gospel that shouts, "He is with you. He is in you!" (John 14:17).

Every great secret makes one poor, it seems. Like a powerful sexual encounter, it cannot be shared and therefore it cannot be understood or valued by others. As a result, it is almost always misunderstood, especially by those who have not yet discovered their own secret or found their own "private room." The secret of divine intimacy is by definition unshareable, ineffable, and mysterious even to the one who enjoys it. It makes you great, but it also makes you very lonely, and often the subject of cruel accusations, comparisons, and spiritual competition, as we see in Peter here.

⸺

I can actually imagine Jesus' words first spoken to one like John, and to every person who has ever experienced the election and elation of divine chosenness: "Go to your own private room [read "intimate place"], where you must shut the door, and pray to your Father in that secret place [read "unshareable experience"], and your Father who sees all that is done in that secret place will reward you" (Matthew 6:6).

In other words, don't expect reward from outside or from others for mystic or religious experience. In fact, it would be quite dangerous if you got it. I tell holy people who come to me to "pray for one good humiliation every day," and then I tell them "to keep careful watch over your reaction to those humiliations." That is the only way you can avoid spiritual grandiosity and know that you are seeking God and not just yourself. The reward must be entirely inherent and interior.

Being a beloved son will not make you fit in, but in fact will make you an outsider in almost all circles—sometimes even to yourself, as you question your own self-assuredness and doubt your own best moments. Every secret makes one poor and lonely, living alone in rooms of doubt. The doubt that comes from an unshareable ecstasy.

Elijah

Just Enough
to Get Your Attention

He went into a cave and spent the night in it. Then the word of Yahweh came to him saying, "What are you doing here, Elijah?" He replied, "I am filled with jealous zeal for Yahweh Sabaoth, because the sons of Israel have deserted you, broken down your altars and put your prophets to the sword. I am the only one left, and they want to kill me too."

[Then comes the lovely account of Elijah's encounter with God, "not in the wind, not in the earthquake, not in the fire, but in a gentle breeze."]

And when Elijah heard this, he covered his face and went out and stood at the entrance to the cave.

Then a voice came to him, which [again] said, "What are you doing here, Elijah?" He replied, "I am filled with jealous zeal for Yahweh Sabaoth, because the sons of

Israel have deserted you, broken down your altars, and put your prophets to the sword. I am the only one left, and they want to kill me too."

I Kings 19:9-14

Elijah is a mixed blessing, as far as I am concerned. I know he is perhaps the first of the speaking prophets and the symbol of those that follow. But, thank God, we have none of his writings, because I fear they would be a mishmash of self-righteous proclamations, like his words quoted above, which only legitimated his own violence. He, like so much of the biblical revelation, is only halfway there, and half of the truth often ends up being a lie. One moment he appears to be leaping forward into true God consciousness, and the next he has retreated to the most abysmal primitive vengeance. Everyone probably hears him, and uses him, at their own level of human and spiritual development. I am convinced that the message in the gentle breeze was to move Elijah toward a more subtle hearing of God, but he seems to prefer wind, earthquake, and fire. In that, he reveals the potential dark side of every truth speaker. Like Elijah, we also prefer absolutes, drama, and total clarity to any "gentle breezes."

In the haunting portrait of Elijah that we have here, I see both a peaceful and a disturbed man. There is a bit of the fanatic in those eyes and yet also a certain contentment that comes from knowing "the truth." I see the same in many religious and dedicated people. It is a workable peace, even a temporarily usable peace, but it is finally a peace that does not last. It is what the desert fathers called a *pax perniciosa,* or false peace—because it needs too much to be right and is based in the small self. It is first-stage-of-life peace, but not yet the peace of God. God's ravens that feed Elijah have also become a source of arrogance and conceit for him. Whenever God grants individuals personal favors, there is the same risk. God grants self-assurance to the person, which is wonderful, but it too often becomes an ego possession, which is terrible. Elijah has been a gifted man up to now and has enjoyed some considerable spiritual benefits from God. Now we will see what he does with them.

I will not bore or shock you with all the gory details, but it seems that every time old Elijah prophesies, there is a blood-bath *for someone else* (1 Kings 18:40, 15-18, 21:19-24; 2 Kings 1:9-16). The Elijah cycle does not make for nice children's stories—or for truly adult stories, for that matter. It appeals only to people who have left childhood but not yet grown up, which happens to be most people. But I still insist, as the tradition does, that Elijah has part of the message and is partly usable by God, and thus is still called a prophet. God seems to be very humble, very patient, and highly inefficient in history. God uses whatever God can get, it seems, even earthen vessels and "cracked pots." (That is not a cheap pun, but a reference to Paul's metaphor in 2 Corinthians 4:7.) Maybe the reason that the tradition always had Elijah returning again was a deep recognition that he did not get it right the first time!

The parts of the truth that Elijah does have, admittedly in an arrogant way, are these: He enjoys the beginnings of strict monotheism, which is needed to clear out the psychological polytheism that affects all of us. We all have "many gods before us," among which are primarily our own ego and our attachment to our opinions and feelings. The price of the death of these many gods is usually major surgery. Second, Elijah is characterized by what I call "mini-mysticism," which one often sees in early-stage renewal movements and early-stage renewed persons. It is only a start, but they take it for the whole enchilada. We see that mysticism in Elijah's early sojourn in the wadi Cherith (1 Kings 17:2-6) and in the popular passage about "the wind, the earthquake, the fire, and the gentle breeze" (1 Kings 19:9-14). But I submit that he never got the full message from either experience.

The giveaway for me is that Elijah "covered his face with his cloak" and "went outside" after the message of the gentle breeze, and "stood at the entrance of the cave." For me, these are all rather obvious symbols of resistance to the message, not awe before it. I think he was frankly disappointed that God did not work through the wind, earthquake, and fire, which was clearly his preferred method and what he wanted to have validated by God. He remained only "at the entrance" of a much deeper message with his "face covered." He is still "outside" the great mystery.

The second giveaway is that he repeats his self-centered mantra one more time about his own "jealous zeal for God." God has asked him twice, "Why are you here?" Elijah never answers God's question. Like a self-absorbed devotee, he merely justifies his own self-image in obsessive-compulsive style, which is the way we all do it. There is little sense of listening or learning in this man. He is a young "true believer" after his honeymoon religious experience. Naturally he became a hero to early Yahwist religion because he proclaimed its absolute superiority. He was that needed "boundary keeper" for a fledgling religion, and he did indeed return in the person of John the Baptist (Matthew 11:14), who had the same black-and-white worldview of the novice enthusiast. It is apparently a good and even necessary way to begin. I know I did. Our boundaries need to be shored up before they can be let go of. We need to have an ego before we can let go of our ego. Most mature believers that I know today were very conservative and even pious or legalistic in the beginning, but they did not stay that way.

The final giveaway is that the only instruction that Yahweh then gives Elijah is to go and anoint his successor—sort of like when Rome appoints a co-adjutor bishop while you are still alive and kicking. And then Yahweh tells him to go anoint two kings, Hazael and Jehu—which he does not do. That task is finally done by his co-adjutor bishop, Elisha. It feels as if poor Elijah has become a merely "useful idiot" for God. No wonder God has finally to send him offstage in a flaming chariot with blazing horses (2 Kings 2:11). It is probably the only way to get rid of him, and in the manner to which he has become accustomed—not unlike the Greek god Phaeton, who is sent driving his doomed chariot across the heavens. Fundamentalists of all sorts, from Taliban to Zionists to Evangelicals, prefer dramatic, staged, and warrior kinds of imagery.

Jesus says of John the Baptist exactly what I would say about Elijah: "No man born of woman is greater than John the Baptist [or Elijah], but the very least in the kingdom of heaven is greater than [either of them]!" Note also the following verse, which finally makes sense with this interpretation: "Up to the present time, this kingdom of heaven has been subjected to violence, and the violent have been taking it away" (Matthew 11:11-12). When you stop after first-stage experience, it is actually worse than not having any experience at all! On the right, it produces cheap zealotry, rigid young clergy, and radical worldviews; on the left, it makes angry ideologues, single-issue idealists, and secular deconstructionists. Both extremes are outside of love and surrender. The "third way" is always a "narrow gate and hard road that leads to life, which only a few find" (Matthew 7:14). I don't think Elijah was ready for any third way. He had the *one* way.

Prophets are often here to get our attention, but they seldom deserve to keep it. They are the whomp on the side of the head that human nature needs to get started and to move beyond inertia, unconsciousness, and delusion. After that, they are only good for calling us back to essentials and keeping us honest. They are never teachers or guides for the long haul. That role is reserved for pastors like Moses, "priests" like Paul (Romans 15:16), and "good shepherds" like Jesus. In the work of the soul, prophets engineer the path of the fall, while priests and pastors engineer the much longer path of the return.

Yes, the Jews of Jesus' time were still hoping that Elijah would return, based on the final prophecy in the Hebrew Scriptures in Malachi. We seem to want and need drama, and strangely are attracted to violence, even in God. Malachi says that Elijah will return to initiate "an awesome and terrible day—lest I come and strike the land with a curse" (2:23-24). Elijah's job is always to make the dramatic entrance and the dramatic exit, but in fact most of a good life is lived in between those two moments. Yet that very in-between will never open up; liminal space will not be available without some needed winds, earthquakes, and fires to destabilize our complacent souls and our enthroned egos.

We will always need Elijah-moments in our lives. Just don't rest there, because there is no rest there, only self-perpetuating dramas to make us feel alive and significant. What Elijah should have known from those ravens is that he was already alive and significant in the only arena that matters.

oseph

Man of Dreams

Now Joseph had a dream, and he repeated it to his brothers. . . .

They saw him at a distance, and before he reached them they made a plot among themselves to put him to death. "Here comes the man of dreams," they said to one another. "Come on, let us kill him and throw him into a well; we can say that some wild beast devoured him. Then we shall see what becomes of his dreams."

Genesis 37:5, 19-20

An angel of the Lord appeared to him in a dream and said, "Joseph, son of David, do not be afraid to take Mary as your wife, for the child conceived in her is from the Holy Spirit. She will bear a son, and you are to name him Jesus, for he will save his people from their sins."

Matthew 1:20-21

It perhaps surprises or confuses you that I have used texts about the earlier Joseph instead of the one in our picture, who is clearly Joseph, the husband of Mary and the foster father of Jesus. I will try to make some appropriate connections that I think the Scriptures already presumed, and you will see that they are both men of dreams. Perhaps we will also see "what became of their dreams."

Well, the Genesis Joseph, the favorite son of Jacob, first incurred his brothers' envy because of that favored status. After he recovered from his consignment to a deep well, he went on, as we all know, to become a dream-interpreter for the pharaoh of Egypt. Soon he became the pharaoh's chancellor, second in command in the empire, in charge of feeding the people in a time of famine. His job description is rather succinct and all encompassing: "Go to Joseph. He will tell you what to do" (Genesis 41:55). This is surely far more than any good Jewish boy ever dreamed of. It shows how much dreams and dream interpretation were valued in those times. That was well before the Western Enlightenment, when we pretty much consigned ourselves to the left mam-malian brain, which has become much darker than Joseph's well ever was.

I would like to say that Joseph, the husband of Mary, who appears only briefly in Matthew's Gospel, was on some sig-nificant levels being connected with the Joseph all Jews would have known about. I have several reasons for saying this, but they are not provable. Sacred stories can always, and must always, be read on many levels to elicit their full transforming power. So let's try.

Our first Joseph is the favorite son of Jacob, the father of the twelve tribes of Israel. In Jacob's final blessing of his twelve sons, he calls Joseph "the dedicated one among his brothers" (Genesis 49:26). The message of the entire Joseph saga (Genesis 37-50) is probably best summed up at the very end. When his brothers rediscover him in Egypt and are saved by him from famine, they offer themselves to him as slaves. But Joseph says what I think the later Joseph might say to poor King Herod, "'The evil you planned to do to me has by God's design been turned into good, that he might bring about, as indeed he has, the deliverance of a great many people. You do not need to be afraid; I myself will provide for you and your dependents.' In this way he reassured them with words that touched their hearts" (Genesis 50:20-21).

Not only is the main thing we hear about the second Joseph that he had four crucial dreams and had the courage both to interpret them and to follow them (Matthew 1:20; 2:13, 19, 22), but we also see that Joseph is clearly chosen as the new favorite son to be the "grand-father" of a new Israel that we call Christianity—which is exactly the role he has carried out, in my opinion. And just as the first Joseph has a totally generous and nonpunitive attitude toward his brothers, so the second Joseph has the same magnanimity toward Mary—even *before* the dream tells him that she has conceived by the Holy Spirit (Matthew 1:19-20). What is not usually remembered is that Joseph was, in fact, breaking the law in order to "spare her publicly and divorce her informally." Not only is he protective of her; he is also nonprotective of himself! Really quite courageous and loving of him, given the times and expectations.

Deuteronomy 22:20-21 is quite clear on this: an espoused girl who has lost her virginity before marriage "shall be taken to the door of her father's house and her fellow citizens shall stone her to death for having committed an act of infamy in Israel by disgracing her father's house. You must banish this evil from your midst." For some reason, this was never made clear in typical storybook accounts of St. Joseph. Either we did not want to expose Jewish punitive legalism, or we did not want to present Joseph as breaking laws, which probably reveals our own legalism. And by legalism I mean when law is seen as an end in itself, instead of the way that Jesus used laws (e.g., Matthew 12:1-8). Where do you think Jesus first learned his attitude toward law? From Joseph! It was the father who taught the law to his children in first-century Judaism, which is very different from Western Christian practice, where it is usually the mother who teaches.

Joseph continues to hear and trust dreams, and it leads him to take a long journey into Egypt to protect his wife and child. Then he has another dream, which he obeys, returning to Israel. Then a final, often-unnoticed dream tells him not to return to Bethlehem of Judea, because Archelaus is king there, but instead to move to Galilee. They take up residence in Nazareth, and after that we hear no more of Joseph in Matthew's account. I wonder if his impending death is not the bit of sadness that we see in our portrait here. The carpenter wants to protect and provide for his wife and son, which he has already shown us in dramatic ways, but perhaps he knows he has to leave the picture soon and leave both of them to the mercy of family and friends. A widow had no other recourse, and there is no mention of Mary ever marrying again.

I believe that the climax of the first Joseph story could also fittingly be the climax of our second Joseph story. Would-be evils have surely been turned into good because of the dreams and faithfulness of one man. Nothing is allowed to thwart God's plans, but God, in fact, thwarts our poor plans, even those of powerful kings, when God has at least one usable instrument, a "dedicated one among his brothers"

(49:26), "a man of honor" (Matthew 1:19), like Joseph the carpenter. Both Josephs catch and contain our best dreams for full manhood.

So what became of Joseph's dreams? Like Moses, we hear that he was not allowed to walk what would normally be the whole journey. He perhaps died as a very young man. The normal age of betrothal was about eighteen for a man and fourteen for a girl. (Can you imagine a contemporary nineteen-year-old boy showing the dedication and maturity that we see in Joseph?) He was not able to live to see his son come to adulthood, and with appropriate symbolism has always been invoked by Catholics as the patron of "a happy death." How could it not have been happy? He knew that he had listened to the dreams that God had given him. He let those dreams take him to far-off Egypt, just like the first Joseph, and he let them bring him to a new hometown, where he surely had to start all over for a third time. He never enjoyed the worldly power or fame of the chancellor of Egypt, as his namesake had. In fact, he disappears rather quietly and humbly into history. He did save his brothers, just like the first Joseph, but it was after his death, as we will soon see.

$$\frown$$

What was said of one can also be paraphrased of the other: God's designs have turned it all to good, so that Joseph might bring about the deliverance of a great many people (Genesis 50:20). I have frequently observed the statuary and art in churches of the world, and there are two ubiquitous images: the mother with child, the Madonna, and, on the other side, the father with child—Joseph. C. G. Jung says that humans tend to create and reproduce *the images that we need for our own transformation*, and that we are transformed only in the presence of images, not concepts. If this is true, and I think it might be, then the image of this humble man Joseph holding a little child safely next to his heart has healed untold tens of thousands throughout the centuries.

$$\frown$$

For I am convinced, after teaching in many countries and cultures, that what I call "the father wound" might well be the most universal wound on this earth. Fathers going to war, fathers deserting families, fathers not part of single-parent child rearing, fathers working at demanding jobs, fathers emotionally unavailable, alcoholic and wounded fathers, and abusive fathers have made it the exception for the male of the species to pass on his soul and himself to his children. We are largely a fatherless world. We have needed a Joseph, a man we could trust to hold us well—to look at and be healed—"that God might bring about, as indeed he has, the deliverance of a great many people" through the faithful life and image of one man. "In this way, he has reassured us and touched our hearts" (Genesis 50:21), just as the first Joseph did when he received his brothers, who became the twelve tribes of Israel.

That's what became of their dreams.

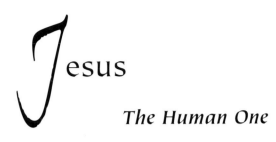

Jesus

The Human One

"From Nazareth?" said Nathaniel. "Can anything good come from that place?"

"Come and see," replied Philip. [And Jesus seemed to reveal something very personal to Nathaniel there.]

To which Nathaniel responded, "You are a son of God, you are the king of Israel."

And Jesus said, "I tell you most solemnly, you will see the heavens laid open upon a human one, and there you will see the angels of God ascending and descending."

John 1:46, 49, 51

I like this particular passage, because Jesus quickly contrasts Nathaniel's effusive praise with what he prefers to call himself, "a son of the human." This is by far the most common term that Jesus uses of himself: a child of here, one of us, an everyman, a human one (*ben ʾādām* is used seventy-nine times!), vicarious humanity, the corporate and victorious person, the new humanity—given to us as model and reconciler of heaven and earth. Jesus offers himself as the archetypal human, while we concentrate, like Nathaniel, on pushing him higher into the heavens as the Nicene Creed's "very God of very God." Why don't we just accept his lead? Maybe "the heavens will be laid open" for us too, in this counterintuitive move, and we will see "angels ascending and descending upon the human one" (John 1:51).

Right after Jesus' "ascension into heaven," almost as an immediate corrective, two men in white said to the first disciples, "Why are you standing here looking into the sky?" (Acts 1:11). But we have been looking into the sky ever since and have largely missed the primary point and momentum of

God in Christ. We don't really like or trust "incarnation" that much. It puts everything too close to home, and we have to take ourselves, our bodies, and this earth more seriously than we really care to. We would rather just be pious, spiritual, or "nice" Christians. Western civilization ends up like the Russian astronauts in space, "God is not up here," they said, with both cynicism and obvious disappointment. God will never be up there, for us, if God is not first of all down here. "As below, so above" or "Thou art That" is the discovery of every mystic and seer. Jesus named the same mystery in the prayer he gave us, "on earth as it is in heaven." Only then is it one coherent universe. Only then do we begin to belong.

One way that we can ignore practical heresy is to condemn it elsewhere or in theory, a strange twist on the old scapegoat mechanism. In the early centuries, the church condemned the heresy of Monophysitism, which claimed that Christ had only one nature and that it was divine. The church insisted, rightly, that Jesus had two natures, human and divine, which were united in his one person—a much harder position to hold or prove. But for most purposes, the practical church has always been Monophysite! We don't take Jesus' human nature seriously at all, and we think even less that there could really be two natures together in one person!

The proof for this is the glaring fact that most of our people have not been able to put it together within themselves. We are sons of earth and daughters of heaven ourselves. On us the angels of God also ascend and descend, just as they did on Jesus. If we can't put it together after centuries of reflecting on Jesus, the living icon of the same, there is little chance we will be able to see the same mystery in ourselves or honor it in others. John of the Cross puts it this way: "This is the great delight of awakening: to know the creature through God and not God through the creature [although that is also possible]; to know the effect through the cause and not the cause through the effect. To know the creature is secondary. To know the cause is essential" (*The Living Flame of Love* 4.5). Thus Jesus is called "the firstborn of all creation" (Colossians 1:15), who makes us "partners in his triumphant parade" (2 Corinthians 2:14). We are all part of a great parade about which we know little, it seems. The essential gospel has not been proclaimed very well. We prefer to doubt both Jesus' incarnation and our own. It is, frankly, just *too* much.

For a monotheistic religion to place a "human one" in the transcendent space reserved for the divine was a dramatic, if not blasphemous, juxtaposition (first hinted at in Daniel 7:13). It is exactly this juxtaposition that Jesus affirms and personally identifies with in constantly calling himself "the human one," while never denying his divine sonship. He holds the unthinkable tension that we deny. In most practical terms, Jesus never once told us to worship him, but he told us many times to "follow him" and to "worship God" (Matthew 4:10). We can only imitate or follow Jesus if we are first of all *like* him, rather than different from him. We worshiped him a bit too easily, and we thereby lost most of his power to recover for us the full face and dignity of our humanity. That is quite a loss. In fact, it is the ultimate loss.

We are not human beings trying to become spiritual. That task has already been done for us by our initial creation as "images of God" (Genesis 1:26). We are already spiritual beings. That is God's gift. Our desperate and needed task, the one we have not succeeded at very well after all these centuries, is *how to become human!* Jesus literally turns religion on its head. He is always moving down, descending into the fully human, identifying freely with our tragic and finite situation. We miss him entirely when we are always running up the down staircase. Our task is to follow and imitate him, not offer him incense, titles, and shrines that he never once asked for. Again, all we need to do is take his lead. Most of the world is so tired of "spiritual people." We would be happy just to meet some real human beings. They always thrill the heart, just as he did.

The allusion used by Jesus in the passage from John's Gospel at the beginning is the lovely story of Jacob/Israel, who has a dream of "a ladder between heaven and earth, with angels ascending and descending" (Genesis 28:12). He ecstatically says, "Truly, God is in this place and I never knew it! How awe-inspiring this place is! This is nothing less than

the house of God. This is the gate of heaven" (28:16-17).
And Jacob places a stone there to mark the ordinary spot
where heaven and earth came together for him, and he
names it Bethel, House of God. Jacob has not gone to an official sanctuary. He has found his distinct and original shrine
"in this place that I never knew!" Remember, for a Jewish person to think that God was in a place other than the tent of
meeting or the temple in Jerusalem was almost an abomina-
tion. Normally the prophets railed against and toppled these
"standing stones," which were considered pagan. But
Yahweh was always making The Presence available in new
and surprising places, it seems, usually in nonreligious
places such as bushes, breezes, and bodies. Like Jacob, we
continue to say, "and I never knew it!"

I am utterly convinced that Jesus did not intend to found "a
religion" at all, much less an imperialistic religion in competition with any other religion. *Jesus is a universal message of
vulnerability that all religions need to meet God authentically, in
order to maintain their own humanity and to keep from destroying*

one another. Jesus came to make a confounding statement about *us*, and we have avoided that message by trying to make profound statements about *him*—statements about which we never all agree and never will agree, but merely argue. Then to top it all off, we Christians cannot ourselves even share a common table of love until we agree on certain doctrinaire propositions. It feels like a catch-22. This is getting humanity nowhere and has made the Christian message anything but admirable, common ground, or the "firstfruits of the Spirit." Perhaps Simone Weil summed it up best, "The tragedy of Christianity is that it came to see itself as replacing other religions instead of adding something to all of them."

God comes to us disguised as our life, which seems to be the last place we want God to be. It is all too ordinary, mundane, fleshy, and unspiritual. It is just "me" and just "you" and just daily life. It is both the perfect hiding place and the perfect revelation place for the Holy One. "What good can come from that place?" Nathaniel says. And Jesus replies,

"Come and see!" By allowing himself to be taken to "the commonplace," the ordinary, to "Our Town," he discovers his soul unveiled, through a moment of such intimacy that even we are not privy to it. It is merely a human disclosure and encounter "under a fig tree" that brings Nathaniel to conversion. No mention of sanctuary, sacrament, or the sacred whatsoever. Until all of life becomes sacramental, the signs in churches don't usually go very deep. There is no readiness to receive them. I can see why Dietrich Bonhoeffer used that shocking phrase in describing our religion in the future. He called it "religionless Christianity."

The spiritual genius and daring of Jesus are that he finds God in the most universal place of all. He absolutely levels the playing field. *He finds God where the suffering is!* Which is everywhere, on both sides of every war, inside every group and religion, and God is nothing that any group can take to itself as an ego possession, even if they be a Syro-Phoenician woman, a Roman centurion, a Samaritan leper, a woman caught in adultery, drunkards and tax-collectors. There is no spiritual loyalty test going in the ministry of Jesus. Not a single one of his healings or exorcisms depends on worthiness—just naked humanity responding to naked humanity. This is a religion that can unite the world and indeed "save the world." Jesus makes it so simple and absolutely clear, but we are still scandalized by this seeming reductionism and oversimplification. We like systems of loyalty and worthiness. We want religion and religion more abundantly, it seems. Jesus wants real life for real people, and he knows that all true life is one and the same—because he has passed through the shadow and the disguise of death: "He is risen from death, he has gone ahead of you into Galilee. It is there that you will see him. Now I have told you" (Matthew 28:7).

So I cannot give up on Jesus, nor am I even tempted to. He holds it all together for me: heaven and earth, human and divine, male body and female soul, power and powerlessness, all hanging between a good and a bad thief, which are the two parts of me. Jesus, especially in the icon of the cross, is a collision of necessary opposites. He is the great bridge builder, and that great bridge has yet to be built for most people I know and most cultures I have visited.

The authentic foundation of all true religion is the rediscovery of the defaced image of God inside of the human person, inside of *this* world, in what will always feel like the naked and empty *now*. This is the ladder to heaven, and it is everywhere.

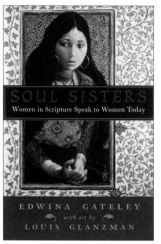